A Heavenly Conversation
One Night Before Christmas

*Whatever is good and perfect is a gift
coming down to us from God our Father,
who created all the lights in the heavens.
He never changes or casts a shifting shadow.*

James 1:17, NLT

A Heavenly Conversation
One Night Before Christmas

Wonder-filled Journey to Christmas, Easter & Beyond

WRITTEN & DESIGNED BY

Jennifer Lynn Heck

Pennsauken, New Jersey

BookBaby
7905 N. Crescent Blvd.
Pennsauken, NJ 08110
www.bookbaby.com

Printed in the United States of America

ISBN: 978-1-09830-214-6

Second Edition

With much gratitude
I dedicate this book to Peggy Heck,
my precious mother and dear friend.
All my life, she has helped me
in countless ways to use God's gifts
for His glory and to encourage people.
Peggy beautifully demonstrates
an intimate relationship with
God the Father, Son and Holy Spirit.

Lord, you are my God;
I will exalt you and praise your name,
for in perfect faithfulness
you have done wonderful things,
things planned long ago.
Isaiah 25:1

Contents

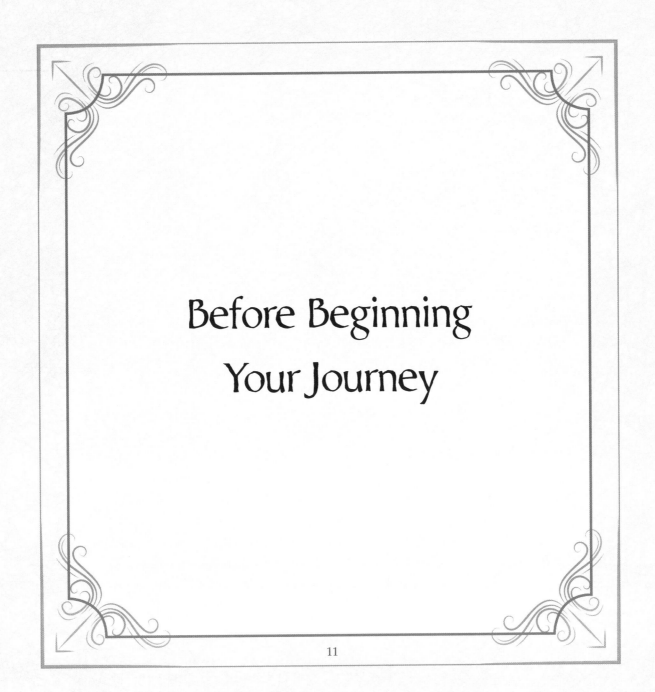

Before Beginning

Your Journey

If the very first Christmas
had not happened,
there would be no Easter.
Without Easter,
humanity would be
hopeless and eternally lost.
Therefore, the significance
and celebration of
Christmas is crucial.

Come along on a wonder-filled journey
to Christmas, Easter and beyond

Shortly before Christmas 2001, I recalled my lifelong fascination with God coming to Earth and pondered the significance of Christ's birth. I felt compelled to write a story telling of his journey from heaven.

The title *A Heavenly Conversation One Night Before Christmas* came to me after I wrote the story's poetic introduction and conclusion. The bookend sections reminded me of the famous poem *'Twas the Night Before Christmas,* written in the early 1800s as a Christmas present for two little girls. In that story, one sleepy yet excited family awaits the much anticipated arrival of jolly Santa Claus with a sleigh full of gifts.

In *A Heavenly Conversation One Night Before Christmas,* I share in joyful wonderment the story of God giving one Christmas present to all people around the entire world. From this one gift, all other blessings flow!

Reader Ages & Backgrounds

✍ The main story begins on page 17. I wrote and designed this story to be meaningful to a broad group of individuals—preteens to senior adults who are familiar with Christianity.

✍ After the main story, there is a separate section titled "Story Snapshots in Pictures." It provides key points of the main story and a foundational understanding of Christianity.

There are three specific groups of people who will particularly benefit from reading the "snapshot" section: people exploring a spiritual faith; people new to the Christian faith; and older elementary children.

Writing Style of the Book

The Bible identifies God as Father, Son and Holy Spirit. The one true God amazingly chooses to interact with humanity in distinct ways. This unique 3-in-1 existence is misunderstood by many people, and it poses a barrier for others.

In an attempt to help people develop a deep appreciation for the awesomeness of God, I wrote this Christmas story as a conversation between the Father, Son and Holy Spirit in heaven before the very first Christmas sometime in eternity past.

Within an hour, you will experience a wonder-filled journey from God's heavenly throne to the creation of the universe; fall of Satan and angels; Garden of Eden; birth, death, resurrection and ascension of Jesus Christ; arrival of the Holy Spirit; and Christ's victorious second coming to sovereignly reign as King of kings and Lord of lords.

A Heavenly Conversation One Night Before Christmas is based on the Bible, which is God's message to humanity (see 2 Timothy 3:16-17). Some of the dialogue in this story includes direct quotes from the Bible. Instead of interrupting the conversation's flow to note the references, I listed them in the appendix for your personal study.

My Gift and Prayer for You

Over the years, as my faith continued to grow, the story and design of *A Heavenly Conversation One Night Before Christmas* also expanded. After nearly two decades of hoping to publish this book, I am filled with joyful gratitude that you are now reading it.

As Christmas and Easter approach, may you experience the real meaning of these two holidays in a fresh and vibrant way. And, even after they have passed, it is my heartfelt prayer that the timeless message of this book will transform you every day throughout the year and forever!

Joyfully in Jesus,

Jennifer

P.S. Throughout the years, a variety of seeds sown into my life influenced the writing of this book (see the appendix).

Written in a unique style,
this book tells the
wonderful story of
God giving people
the greatest
Christmas present
sometime in eternity past

A Heavenly Conversation

One Night Before Christmas

One night before Christmas

Sometime in eternity past,

Not a creature could yet know

God gave His greatest gift at last.

In the beginning God

created the heavens and the earth.

The earth was formless and empty,

and darkness covered the deep waters.

And the Spirit of God was hovering

over the surface of the waters.

Then God said, "Let there be light,"

and there was light.

Genesis 1:1-3, NLT

God the Father:

Jesus, the moment will soon arrive for the next step in our plan from eternity past to be fulfilled.

Obedient Son, it is almost time for you to leave your heavenly throne and go to planet Earth.

God the Son:

Abba Father, I eagerly await your direction.

God the Holy Spirit:

Jesus, before you make your much anticipated departure, look at everything that you, the Father and I created in the universe. It pleased us and we agreed it was very good.

God the Father:

We made human beings in our image and gave them dominion over the earth.

In the perfect garden, we walked and talked with Adam and Eve. More than anything, we desired for them to love us with the free will that we gave them.

God the Son:

I remember the fateful moment, Father, when they chose instead to listen to the deceptive words of the devil.

Lucifer was one of the most beautiful of all our heavenly angels, whom we also created and gave free will. Yet, in the pride of his heart, he desired to become our equal. Therefore, we cast this wayward angel out of heaven. In his fierce rebellion, Lucifer swept away a third of the angels and they became his demonic forces in the world.

By following the enticements of Satan the devil, Adam and Eve damaged their relationship with us. They chose not to trust us and our protective ways, which we designed for their ultimate good, freedom and pleasure.

Oh Father and Holy Spirit, it broke our heart to banish the first man and his wife from our presence!

As a result of their disobedience, decay and destruction came into the world. Sin started having cascading effects throughout the centuries—disasters in nature, fear, guilt, shame, loneliness, conflict, hatred, wars, sorrow, pain, disease and death.

God the Holy Spirit:

Yes Jesus, we grieved greatly over the separation from the children we created.

Again and again, we sent our servants to them. The prophets proclaimed, "Each of you must turn from your wicked ways and reform your actions; do not follow other gods to serve them."

But, our people did not pay attention or listen.

God the Father:

To this very day, many people still choose to live in ways that seem right to them. Satan roams the Earth blinding the minds of our loved ones to the truth. The devil also enslaves people to all kinds of evil and numbs them with apathy. Satan is relentless, even though he knows we have already destined him and his demons to eternal torment.

People fall prey to the devil's cunning lies. They think it is possible to earn their way into heaven, which they believe saves them. Each person has a different idea about what it means to be *good enough*. This is in itself prideful, which is the root of sin. Individuals can never become righteous by keeping the law or a set of standards. This is simply impossible because every person inherits a sinful, imperfect nature.

Just like they inherit hundreds of traits from their parents, people also have no control over inheriting a sinful nature. Look at precious little children—they do not need to be taught how to want and get their own way. All people, born into a fallen world, are already infected by the deadly sin disease.

God the Son:

Merciful Father and Holy Spirit, we sovereignly know that this deceptive struggle is inside people around the world, and has been throughout all time.

Due to rebellion in its various forms, people's decision to live in opposition to us results in a vast chasm of separation. But with intense compassion, we are eager to close the gap and welcome them back with open arms. It is our desire for everyone to come to repentance and we wait patiently for those who choose to do so.

In the very moment individuals accept our gift of salvation, we rescue them from the devil's kingdom of darkness, sin and death. We transfer them into our kingdom of light, righteousness and new life. Even before we created the world, I already purchased their freedom and forgiveness of sins.

We delight in redeeming people's lives marred by sin. Because we greatly love individuals, we replace their stony, stubborn heart with a tender, responsive heart.

We also give them an undivided heart and put a new spirit within them. This enables them to love and follow us—no longer out of legalism, but rather out of joyful obedience with all their heart, soul, mind and strength.

God the Father:

Jesus and Holy Spirit, let us now return to our conversation about sending many prophets to help individuals find their way back to us.

Four hundred years have passed since we last spoke to people. The remnant who believe the truth is becoming weary, waiting for the promised Savior in a land of ever increasing wickedness and oppression.

Therefore Jesus, now is the time for you to go down to Earth on a rescue mission. Our tender mercy and boundless love compels us to do so.

As with any time in history, many people will continue choosing to live in darkness rather than turn to the light of truth. Jesus, they will refuse to believe that you are the one true God. But you must stand firm in the face of opposition and persecution. Remember why you are being sent.

Son, the Holy Spirit will be upon you to preach good news to the poor, bind up the brokenhearted, proclaim freedom for the captives, and announce the year of our favor and the day of our vengeance.

You will also give individuals beauty instead of ashes, gladness instead of mourning and a spirit of praise instead of despair.

God the Holy Spirit:

Faithful Son, I have searched throughout the Jewish nation to find a teenage virgin girl whose heart is pure and who is obedient in our sight.

Look, Jesus! Look, right down there. There she is—her name is Mary.

Very soon I will envelop her with my presence and power. I will transport you from reigning at the right hand of Father God and place you inside Mary's womb as a tiny, helpless baby.

This is the perfect way for you to become fully human, while retaining your total divinity. You will be known as both the Son of Man and the Son of God.

Our glorious angels will announce your long-awaited birth to our chosen human servants: your mother Mary, stepfather Joseph and lowly shepherds. I will place a brilliant star in the sky, which will guide the way for prestigious Magi to come worship you.

Jesus, when the appointed time arrives for your birth, your earthly parents will be traveling on a journey. Being weary from walking and riding a donkey in rough terrain, they will seek lodging. Yet the only available shelter will be a smelly stable.

Your newborn cry will be heard by Mary, Joseph and all of heaven. Your first cradle will be a feeding trough for animals—animals that you created.

God the Son:

Holy Spirit, although I am equal with you and the Father in divine nature, I have been willing from eternity past to humble myself by becoming a servant made into the likeness of a man.

Abba Father, I place my trust in you. I will speak only what you tell me to say. I will declare your name to our people. While living in their midst, I will sing your praises. Then when you tell me it is time, my Father, I will become obedient to the ultimate purpose for which you are sending me.

I will destroy the work of Satan, who holds people in bondage. Though no sin will ever be found in me, I will lay down my life as payment for the sin that separates every individual from us. I will die like a criminal to set them free from the deadly eternal consequences.

The multitudes of gods that have been conceived and worshiped by human beings, throughout all time, offer to save their followers only if they *do* a list of things to earn it. I am coming down from heaven to proclaim eternal salvation has already been *done* for them through me.

Faithful Father and Holy Spirit, you promise to give this glorious gift to everyone who genuinely receives it by faith.

God the Father:

This has been our plan all along.

We began revealing it to Adam and Eve in the Garden of Eden. When they entered into sin, it made them aware of having guilty consciences and being ashamed of their naked bodies. They tried hiding from our presence.

Yet even after they disobeyed us, we showed that we still loved them. We killed an innocent animal to clothe them with its skin. Through this object lesson, we started teaching humanity that the blood of a blameless sacrifice covers and forgives sin.

Throughout all time, we choose to cover people's sins with our righteousness. Jesus, you will become known as the Lamb who was slain. Your bloody death will become the perfect and final sacrifice for sin.

People who have ears to hear and hearts to believe, through-out all nations and in every generation, will understand that it is by our grace they are saved through faith in you.

Son of Man, we love individuals so much that we have given them both the first and the last sacrifice to cover their sin-stained soul. We simply ask them to sincerely accept our gift of salvation—which means eternal forgiveness of sins, freedom from death and a new life full of dynamic purpose.

God the Holy Spirit:

Jesus, once you willingly become the final sacrifice, the Father and I cannot be in your presence. This is because all of the sin—from every generation in time—will be heaped upon you.

You will be temporarily isolated from us and we will all experience excruciating pain over that separation!

Son of Man, in your agony you will cry out to the Father, "Abba, why have you forsaken me? Everything is possible for you. Please take this cup of suffering away from me. Yet I want your will, not my own will to be done. I am ready to finish what you sent me to Earth to accomplish."

God the Father:

Precious Son, in your humanness you will suffer horrendous pain. You will be rejected by family and betrayed by friends. Crowds will shout, "Crucify him!" You will be despised and condemned by religious leaders. Roman soldiers will mock and spit on you. They will take pleasure in flogging you over and over, ripping open your skin.

Jesus, hate-filled men will beat you and strike your head repeatedly with a staff. You will be stripped and blindfolded. A crown of thorns will be mashed into your head; nails will be hammered through your hands and feet; and a spear will be pierced into your side. You will hang on a splintered wooden cross for six agonizing hours, placed between two convicted criminals.

God the Holy Spirit:

As the Father and I watch these events unfolding from heaven, our heart will break with indescribable anguish.

Jesus, you will be disfigured beyond any human likeness. Right before you take your final breath, you will shout, "Father, I place my life in your hands!" Then, your crucified body will be placed inside a guarded tomb.

Son of God, there will be a violent earthquake on the third day. An angel will roll back the stone and announce that you are no longer in the grave. Jesus, you will triumphantly rise from the dead—just as you foretold!

Because you conquered death, Jesus, the Father gives you authority and power to raise everyone from the dead who places his or her faith in you.

God the Son:

After my resurrection, I will spend additional time on Earth. A crowd of more than five hundred people will witness that I am alive. They will interact with me in my new body. I will also enjoy eating and talking with my family, friends and disciples.

Forty days later, after preparing them for what is to come, I will ascend through the clouds into heaven. Two angelic messengers will proclaim that the faithful Father will send me a second time to Earth at his appointed time in the future.

God the Father:

Jesus, at your first coming to the people we lovingly created, you will take the form of a helpless baby and only a few people will know of your arrival.

At your second coming, you will arrive suddenly as the victorious king and conquering warrior. The entire world will know that it is you coming to establish our kingdom. All people will hear a loud command, the archangel's voice and our trumpet call. Jesus, you will descend from heaven through the clouds. The sky will be filled with your glorious presence and an army of angels will accompany you.

Son of God, you will eliminate mourning, crying, pain and death. You will keep your promise to make all things new!

God the Holy Spirit:

Jesus, before the Father sends you to Earth the second time, he will send me after your resurrection and ascension.

Since you and the Father will be together again in heaven, I desire to go to the precious people we created, continuing to offer them our incomparable mercy and grace. Whether they know it or not, all people need my presence in their lives.

God the Son:

Spirit of Truth, with you being in the entire world, billions of people will have the capacity to understand truth. You will convict individuals of sin, righteousness and judgment.

If people allow you to help them daily, they will discover you are a priceless treasure—worth more than all the gold and jewels.

God the Holy Spirit:

Faithful Son, I promise to live inside everyone who genuinely declares that you are Lord and believes in his or her heart that Father God resurrected you from the dead. My constant presence within individuals is a guarantee that they will receive everything we promise to give them.

I empower people to put to death their self-centered, worldly and unforgiving nature. I equip them with spiritual weapons to conquer the evil schemes that Satan hurls against humanity.

Jesus, I assist people in communicating with you and the Father. I give them special abilities to serve other people. I counsel individuals when they are confused and provide wisdom in making decisions. I comfort and heal them during times of pain and brokenness.

The fruitful evidence of my abundant life within people is that they experience and share love, joy, peace, patience, kindness, goodness, faithfulness, gentleness and self-control. I give them wonderful purpose and contentment—comparable to absolutely nothing the world has to offer.

God the Father:

Holy Spirit and Jesus, as a reminder of our plan from eternity past, it has been good for us to have this heavenly conversation one night before the very first Christmas.

Obedient Son, remember that you are going to Earth on a rescue mission because we lavishly love all people. Show them, through your life and death, that every person has precious value and worth. Our heart's desire is for all individuals to have a fulfilling and close relationship with us.

Jesus, are you ready to experience life as a human in order to restore the broken relationship with our people—those who have eyes of faith willing to see into the heavenly kingdom?

God the Son:

YES, I AM!

For the joy and suffering set before me, I am ready to become the Christmas gift from which all other blessings flow.

But when the **time** arrived

that was **set** by God the Father,

God sent his **Son**,

born among us of a woman,

born under the conditions of the law

so that he might **redeem** those of us

who have been kidnapped by the law.

Thus we have been set **free**

to experience our rightful heritage.

Galatians 4:4-5, MSG

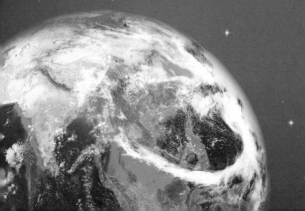

*E*verything happened

Just as L<small>ORD</small> God said it would;

His Word one night before

Christmas forever stood!

Story Snapshots
in Pictures

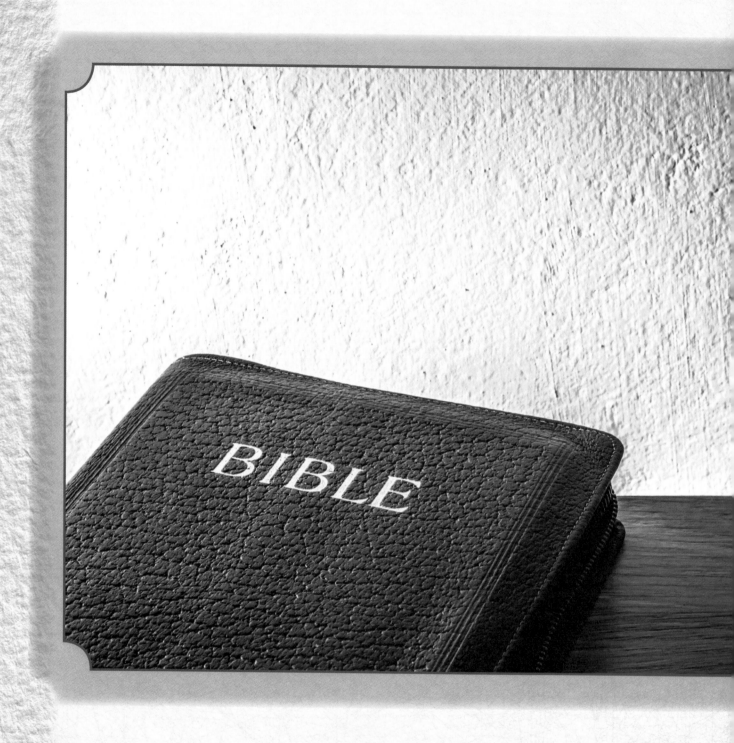

The Bible

The **Bible** is the foundation of the story *A Heavenly Conversation One Night Before Christmas*.

Do you know about the Bible? It is a very special book. It introduces people to God. He created everything and oversees all things. God cares very much for you and for every person in the entire world.

The Bible tells how the universe began. It records world events in history and prepares people for what is to come in the future.

The Bible describes the nature of human beings. It shares how you can find meaningful purpose in life. The Bible also tells you how to have eternal life in heaven.

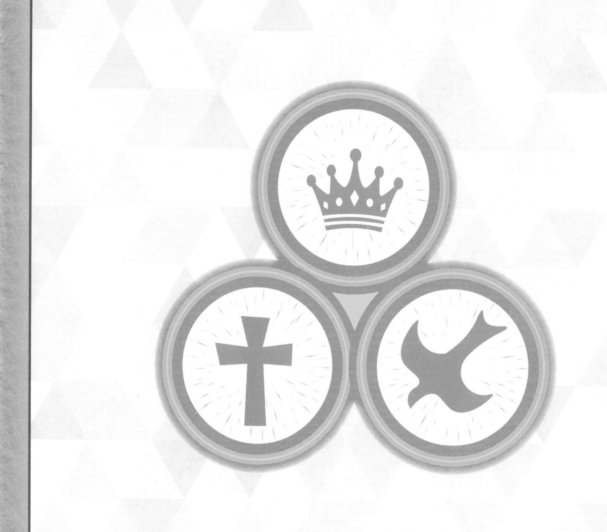

God is the divine being who created the entire universe and everything in it. He has no beginning and no end. God is not an impersonal force. Rather, he knows people individually and wants to be involved in their daily lives.

God is so big that he can hold the heavens and earth in one of his hands. At the same time, God cares deeply for every person throughout all time and eternity.

The Bible identifies God as three divine persons: Father, Son and Holy Spirit.

God's unique 3-in-1 existence can be difficult to understand. A simple definition is that the one true God chooses to interact with people in distinct ways. Some of God's characteristics are:

Present everywhere at the same time

All knowing • All powerful • Above all false gods

Perfect • Loving • True • Just • Good • Righteous

Angry at evil • Mighty • Forgiving • Holy

Generous • Joyful • Kind • Patient • Faithful

In the beginning

God created the heavens and the earth. These are the opening words of the Bible. It is important to realize that everything in the universe is not the result of an unknown cosmic big bang or as stated by the theory of evolution.

The heavens and the earth have a powerful and intelligent designer. Let's read more about how the Bible describes the creator God.

"The heavens proclaim the glory of God. The skies display his craftsmanship. Day after day they continue to speak; night after night they make him known.

"Look up into the heavens. Who created all the stars? He brings them out like an army, one after another, calling each by its name. Because of his great power and incomparable strength, not a single one is missing."
(Genesis 1:1, Psalm 19:1-2, Isaiah 40:26, NLT)

God created the angels in heaven. There are too many angels to count. Some angels praise God all the time. Some serve in heaven's army. Other angels are messengers to people.

When he created the angels, God gave them the ability to make their own decisions. Lucifer was one of the most beautiful of all the angels. He became filled with pride, which means that he had an exaggerated opinion of who he was and what he could do. Lucifer chose to rebel against his creator. He wanted to be like God.

Because God could no longer keep him in heaven, Lucifer was thrown down to Earth. Lucifer became Satan the devil, who is the leader of fallen angels. Satan is the source of sin, evil and destruction in the world.

Always remember: the devil is not equal with God. God created him as a good angel. Satan chose to rebel and he became a demon, which is an evil angel.

God created everything in the universe. God made light, water, animals and plants. God also created all people.

The names of the first man and first woman were Adam and Eve. God built a beautiful home for them. It was called the Garden of Eden. God made the perfect garden for their enjoyment. He walked and talked with Eve and Adam in the garden.

God gave them the ability to make their own decisions, including knowing and loving him. This gift of free will enabled them to disobey God's one and only warning. Adam and Eve were told not to eat the fruit from the tree of the knowledge of good and evil.

Because God greatly loves people, he offers wonderful freedom within protective boundaries. Since he knows everything, God knew what would happen if Adam and Eve disobeyed him.

***

Satan found a way to show his fierce anger for God. When he saw that God loved Adam and Eve very much, Satan decided to tempt them to disobey God.

Adam and Eve listened to Satan, rather than trusting God. They ate the fruit from the tree of the knowledge of good and evil.

Here's a simple definition of sin: Sin is pridefully choosing to live according to people's standards and desires, rather than believing and obeying God.

The moment Adam and Eve disobeyed God, their sin started affecting the world. The impact of sin is seen across the globe. Creation suffers disasters in nature. Nations wage war against other nations. People experience guilt, shame, conflict, fear, loneliness, sorrow, pain, disease and death.

***

God still loved Adam and Eve after they rebelled against him. However, they chose to live the way that pleased their own selves. That one decision created a big gap between God and people.

Since God is perfect in every way, he has always known that people can never bridge the gap by their own efforts. People are not able to do enough good deeds to make up for disobeying God. This is simply impossible because every person inherits a sinful and imperfect nature, something over which they have no control.

Because God greatly loves all people, he gave the ultimate solution. With intense compassion, God left heaven and became a human being to bridge the gap and restore the broken relationship with people.

God the Father sent God the Son to planet Earth. Another name for God the Son is Jesus Christ.

Christmas

is the holiday that remembers and celebrates God the Son coming into the world he created, so that he could rescue people.

At God the Father's appointed time in history, he sent angels to Earth announcing the arrival of God the Son. One of the angels said:

> *Joseph son of David, do not be afraid to take Mary home as your wife, because what is conceived in her is from the Holy Spirit. She will give birth to a son, and you are to give him the name Jesus, because he will save his people from their sins.* (Matthew 1:20-21)

On the night Jesus was born, many angels filled the sky. They told poor shepherds how to find God the Son. The shepherds left their sheep and found Jesus lying in a manger—a feeding trough for stable animals.

God also placed a brilliant star over the place where Jesus was born. The Star of Bethlehem guided the way for wealthy wisemen to come worship the infant king.

Easter

is the holiday that remembers and celebrates God the Son choosing to suffer and die, so that he could become the substitute to forever pay the penalty of people's sin and give them wonderful eternal life.

In divine perfection, God the Son lived as a man on Earth for thirty-three years. He served humanity with truth and grace. Then, Jesus Christ willingly shed his human blood for the joy of restoring the broken relationship between God and people.

Jesus hung on a wooden cross for six painful hours. Through his sacrificial death, God the Son forever broke the bondage of sin. Jesus conquered Satan, who is the number one enemy of all people.

Jesus
Christ died and his body was placed in a sealed tomb, securely guarded by soldiers.

On the third day, God the Father breathed new life into Jesus and raised him from the dead. God resurrected Jesus to let everyone know that he accepted Christ's death as the final payment for sin.

On the very first Easter morning, God the Son removed the curse of sin and death for people. God promises you will live forever with him in heaven if you accept his gift of salvation.

Do you confess that you are a sinner, who chooses to live by your standards? Are you ready to ask God to forgive you? If so, Jesus Christ patiently waits to be your Savior and give you a fantastic new life.

The Holy Spirit came to Earth after Jesus Christ was raised from the dead.

For forty days, Jesus interacted with more than five hundred people. After he finished preparing them for what is to come, God the Father took Jesus back into heaven through the clouds. Then he sent the Holy Spirit.

The Bible describes the Holy Spirit as fire, wind and a dove. If you truly accept Jesus Christ as your Savior and Lord, the Holy Spirit comes to live inside you as your constant helper and comforter.

God the Holy Spirit enables you to have love, joy, peace, patience, kindness, goodness, faithfulness, gentleness and self-control.

If you allow God to help you every day, you will discover that the Holy Spirit is a priceless treasure—worth more than all the world's gold and jewels.

In the future God the Son will

come to Earth again. At Jesus Christ's first coming, he took the form of a helpless baby and only a few people knew of his arrival.

At his second coming, Jesus will arrive suddenly. He will be the victorious king and conquering warrior. The entire world will know that it is God coming to establish his kingdom.

When Jesus Christ returns in majesty and glory, four of his names will be revealed: FAITHFUL AND TRUE, WORD OF GOD, KING OF KINGS, and LORD OF LORDS.

Riding a white horse, Jesus will come down from heaven through the clouds. The sky will be filled with his bright presence and an army of angels. God the Son will eliminate sadness, crying, pain and death. He will keep his promise to make all things new!

After Finishing
Your Journey

After finishing your wonder-filled journey...

Reflect on the following. Does it require greater control and power to "restrain" or "unleash" what's inside you? What about how it applies to God?

Before the first Christmas, God the Son willingly humbled himself by becoming a helpless baby. He *restrained* part of his majestic self in order to save the people he lovingly created.

Before the first Easter, God the Son willingly wore a crown of thorns and hung on a wooden cross. Again, he *restrained* part of himself—not unleashing his power to escape suffering in order to save the people he lovingly created.

When Jesus Christ returns wearing a crown as the sovereign king, he will simply *unleash* himself to the world he lovingly created. Nothing and no person will be able to stop him!

What would life be like if God the Father, Son and Holy Spirit decided not to be perfectly balanced in restraining and unleashing his power?

Your Conversation
with God

God the Father gives you

his **mercy** and **grace.**

God the Son gives you

his **forgiveness** of sins

and **new life.**

God the Holy Spirit gives you

his constant **help** and **comfort.**

When you realize how much the God of the universe loves you and what he did for you, there will be a longing in your heart to respond to him.

The Bible provides a guide to begin your relationship with God the Father, Son and Holy Spirit. It is found in Romans 10:9-10 and Acts 2:38.

❶ Declare that Jesus Christ is Lord;
❷ Believe that God raised Jesus from the dead;
❸ Repent of your sins *(confess your sins and turn away from your sinful/selfish desires);*
❹ In the name of Jesus Christ, be baptized for the forgiveness of your sins.

Many parents have their infants sprinkled with water in a church as baptism and/or dedication to God. Although this is meaningful to the family, infants are not capable of making their own decisions.

Baptism is meant to be an obedient response after you accept Jesus Christ as your Lord and Savior. The Bible describes baptism as being immersed into water. God designed baptism to publicly demonstrate your faith and trust in him:

You choose to die to your sins;
Your old life is buried in a watery grave;
God raises you to live a new life forever in Jesus Christ.

$\mathcal{R}$egardless of where you are currently along your spiritual journey, it is my hope that you will want to respond to God the Father, Son and Holy Spirit.

After reading the story *A Heavenly Conversation One Night Before Christmas*, you are now aware of Jesus Christ's sacrificial death and glorious resurrection. God is willing and able to forgive your sins, and to give you eternal life in heaven.

Because of the Holy Spirit's presence, God made a way for you to communicate directly with him. Prayer is the wonderful privilege of having conversations with God—listening, hearing and talking with him. Even though your prayers do not need to be written, feel free to pen a heartfelt message to God on the next page.

Your Conversation with God

APPENDIX

Bible References

Page 21 & 22

John 6:38-40
John 8:27-29
Genesis 1—3

Page 23

Ezekiel 28:11-17
Isaiah 14:12-15
1 John 2:16
Proverbs 16:18
Revelation 12:1-17
Romans 8:19-22

Page 24

Jeremiah 35:15

Page 25

Proverbs 14:12
1 Peter 5:8
2 Corinthians 4:4
Jude 1:6
Revelation 20:1-3,7-10

Romans 3:21-31
Galatians 3:1-14
Ephesians 2:1-10

Page 26

Isaiah 59:1-2
Hosea 11:1-4
Lamentations 3:22-23
Isaiah 54:7-8
1 Timothy 2:3-6
2 Peter 3:8-9
Romans 6:23
Colossians 1:13-14
Ezekiel 11:19-20
Mark 12:30

Page 27

Malachi 3:16-18
Galatians 4:4-5
Hebrews 1:1-3
John 1:1-5,9-14
John 3:16-21

John 17:1-8
John 10:22-33
Luke 4:14-21
Isaiah 61:1-3

Page 28

Luke 1:26-38
Matthew 1:18—2:12
Luke 2:1-20,51-52

Page 29

John 14:6-7
Colossians 2:9
Philippians 2:5-11
Hebrews 2:9-18
1 John 3:8
2 Corinthians 5:20-21
John 10:14-18
Psalm 115:2-8
Jeremiah 2:11-13
1 Peter 1:18-21

Page 30

Revelation 5:6-14
Revelation 13:8
Hebrews 7:23-28
Romans 5:12-21

Page 31-33

Psalm 5:4
Habakkuk 1:13
1 John 1:5
1 John 2:1-2
Matthew 26:36—28:20
Mark 14:32—16:8
Luke 22:39—24:53
John 18:1—21:14
1 Peter 2:21-25
Isaiah 52:14
1 Corinthians 6:14
Galatians 1:1-5

Page 34

1 Corinthians 15:3-8
Acts 1:1-11

Page 35

1 Thessalonians 4:13—5:3
Revelation 19:11-16
Revelation 21:1-5

Page 36

John 14:16-18,26
John 16:7-11
Acts 2:1-41
John 15:26
Proverbs 8:10-11

Page 37

Romans 12:4-8
1 Corinthians 2:9-16
1 Corinthians 12:1-31
Galatians 5:22-23
Ephesians 6:10-18
2 Corinthians 1:20-22

Page 38

1 John 3:1

Page 39

Hebrews 12:2-3

Page 41

Isaiah 14:24,26-27
Psalm 33:11
1 Peter 1:23-25

In the beginning
the Word already existed.
The Word was with God,
and the Word was God.
He existed in the beginning with God.
God created everything
through him, and nothing was created
except through him. . . .
For this is how God loved the world:
He gave his one and only Son, so that
everyone who believes in him
will not perish but have eternal life.
God sent his Son into the world
not to judge the world, but to save the
world through him.

John 1:1-3, 3:16-17, NLT

Bible Passages for Further Study
of God's Wonderful Story

Deuteronomy 4:39

1 Chronicles 16:25-27

Job 11:7-9

Psalm 33:4-15
Psalm 103:8-22
Psalm 139:1-18

Proverbs 3:5-6

Ecclesiastes 3:11

Isaiah 9:6-7
Isaiah 43:25
Isaiah 44:24
Isaiah 46:9-11
Isaiah 53:1-12

Jeremiah 29:11-13
Jeremiah 31:3

Amos 4:13

Micah 7:18-19

Nahum 1:2-7

Zechariah 12:1

Zephaniah 3:17

Matthew 2:1-23

Mark 1:9-13

Luke 3:21-22

John 3:5-8
John 8:42-44

Acts 4:11-12

Romans 6:1-14
Romans 8:1-39
Romans 10:9-13

1 Corinthians 15:20-26,35-57

Galatians 5:13-26

Ephesians 1:3-14

Colossians 1:15-23
Colossians 3:12-17

2 Timothy 3:14-17

Hebrews 1:14
Hebrews 8—9

James 2:19

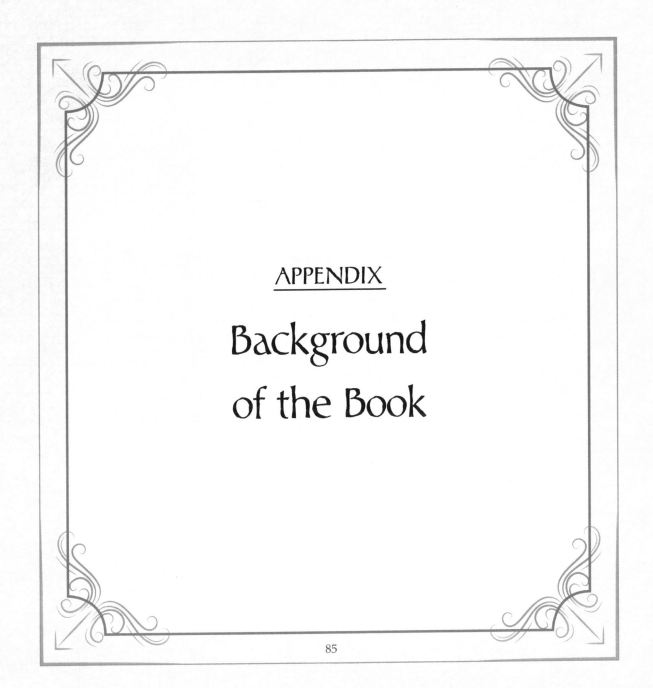

APPENDIX

Background
of the Book

Seeds sown years ago served as fertile soil for the birth of this book

*D*uring my childhood, my parents took me to church regularly where I learned about Father God and Jesus Christ. However, the two churches we attended did not preach about the Holy Spirit.

Yet even as a youngster, it became evident that God's Spirit was working in my life. Without encouragement from anyone, I drew the scene of Christ's birth over and over.

"In amazement, I watched my daughter capture her love for God," recalls Peggy Heck. "Regardless of the time of year, Jenny knelt beside her bed which she used as a desk. With a pad of paper and box of crayons, she drew and wrote about Jesus coming to Earth at Christmas. Jenny spent hours in this kneeling position, even though it was a struggle for her to move her arms and hold a crayon due to being born with cerebral palsy."

Drawing of the nativity by 6-year-old Jennifer Heck

At the age of 12, I accepted Jesus Christ as my Savior. My decision was genuine—confessing and repenting of my sinful nature, asking Jesus into my heart and allowing him to begin transforming my life. During high school and college, Lord God enabled me to achieve much success. However, I still had a hole in my soul that nothing on earth could fill. I realized that Jesus was continuing to knock on my heart's door.

At age 22, I asked Christ Jesus to be the sovereign Lord of my life. It was then that I started experiencing consistent joy and purpose, no longer stifled by *religion* but fulfilled in a daily *relationship* with God.

My faith journey skyrocketed when I joined Southeast Christian Church at the age of 28. It is at this church that I have grown in understanding and deep gratitude of God's glorious nature and his Word (i.e., the Bible). There is no perfect church, because there are no perfect people. However, this church has a 55+ year history of boldly—yet lovingly—preaching, teaching and applying God's Word.

*T*he first event is now known as 9/11. Was it a coincidence, prior to this infamous day in history, that the phone number 911 was established as the urgent number to call for emergencies?

Two powerful events planted more seeds for this book

Like millions of people around the world, I remember exactly where I was at 8:46 the morning of September 11, 2001. Within eighty minutes, three airplanes crashed into key economic and military buildings in the United States of America. Due to the actions of courageous passengers, a fourth plane missed its target and plummeted into a rural field. The horrifying events were quickly discovered to be the result of terrorist hijackers.

Our country mourned for the 3,000 men, women and children who lost their lives and futures in a split second on that fateful day. Rescue workers frantically and tirelessly searched through rubble for weeks. Risking their own lives, these heroes sought to find survivors because they valued the worth of individuals.

On the morning of 9/11, each of us got up and did all the usual things in our daily lives. We were unaware of the impending evil plot already set in motion. It would forever impact thousands of victims, their families, our nation and the world.

Now pause those thoughts as I share the second powerful event I encountered during that same autumn.

One Sunday I attended the evening worship service at my church. A friend invited a young man, Chad Russell, to join him. All three of us were grouped together for a focused time of prayer.

With the enthusiasm of a child and the confidence of a man, Chad boldly declared that four months earlier he was born again into God's kingdom. *[Chad granted me permission to share his testimony.]*

For more than 25 years, Chad thought he was living right by attending church every week and being an overall good guy. However, his life was focused on pursuing a materialistic lifestyle, seeking social status, drinking and sexual immorality.

Through a series of what he called "touches of God," Chad realized he had not been living a good life. By turning away from his self-centered desires and turning toward Jesus, Chad received glorious forgiveness and eternal life. He publicly declared Christ as his Lord and Savior. In response to his new life, Chad was then baptized before the church congregation.

"I was in church my entire life and thought God graded on the curve," he shared with me after the worship service. "Yet I was on a path to hell and I had no idea."

Chad joyfully concluded, "Being a Christian is not a 9 to 5 job or just giving Christ the parts of my life I want him to have. I gave my life to

Christ to be my King. I now know the only way to an eternal future in heaven is through Christ Jesus!"

After meeting this new Christian, Chad and I developed a friendship based on our mutual faith in Jesus Christ.

At that point in my life, I had been a Christian for 24 years. I loved LORD God sincerely and wholeheartedly. I found myself sharing with Chad key aspects of developing a dynamic faith relationship with the God of the universe.

As the Christmas season approached, I thought about how differently Chad would now celebrate the holiday. Strange as it may sound, I also reflected upon September 11's terrorist attacks.

First, I saw spiritual parallels with what heroic workers did trying to rescue survivors and what LORD God did in coming to eternally save people. As God the Son, Jesus Christ humbled and sacrificed himself unto death because he valued the worth of every individual.

Second, I wondered if the people who lost their lives on 9/11 were ready to enter eternity.

Third, I pondered: How can individuals become terrorists? They must be so deceived by Satan and consumed with hatred, believing it is acceptable to murder thousands of people.

With all these reflections lingering in my mind and heart, God stirred me to write a Christmas story. The more I listened to the prompting of the Holy Spirit, the more he expanded the story's scope.

> Rather than only retelling the Bible's account of Jesus Christ's birth, I wanted to help people grasp the significance of this pivotal event in context of the Bible's overarching message for humanity. My Christmas story would share God's amazing love and forgiveness in response to individuals choosing to follow the ways of Satan.

It broke my heart recalling that on 9/11 several thousands of people died, and some of them possibly were not prepared to enter eternity. With this in mind, it was also my desire to write a story that would guide individuals toward having the assurance that they are ready NOW to cross over into eternity.

Over the years, God the Father, Son and Holy Spirit planted all these seeds in me. In his sovereign knowledge, he knew someday the seeds would take root, grow and produce a harvest. Lord God knew that someday he would enable me to write and design this book.

It's news I'm most proud to proclaim, this extraordinary Message of God's powerful plan to rescue everyone who trusts him, starting with Jews and then right on to everyone else!

Romans 1:16, MSG

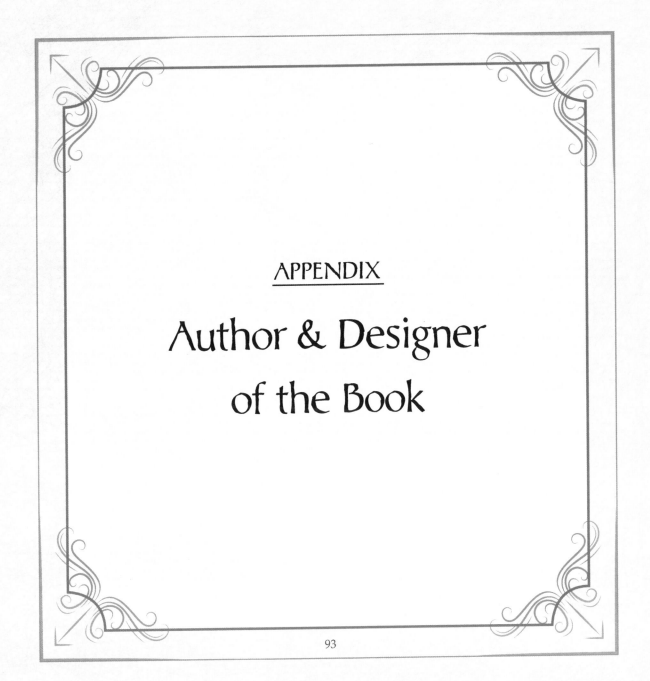

APPENDIX

Author & Designer
of the Book

Jennifer Lynn Heck was born with cerebral palsy. That hasn't stopped her from taking many leaps of faith. It includes seven tandem skydives, one at 15,000 feet.

She passionately believes, "My mission in life is to break barriers between people and build bridges to God. Everyone needs to know Jesus Christ, grow in their faith and use their God-given gifts for his glory."

For nearly thirty years, Jennifer worked as a graphic designer of publications and has written more than 130 articles. Most of the newspaper articles were published in *The Southeast Outlook*, where she served as a columnist for ten years. She is a member of Southeast Christian Church in Louisville, Kentucky.

Jennifer graduated from the University of Louisville with a bachelor's degree in Business Administration. She earned a second bachelor's degree from Johnson Bible College; Knoxville, Tennessee. Her major was the Bible and she specialized in disability ministry.

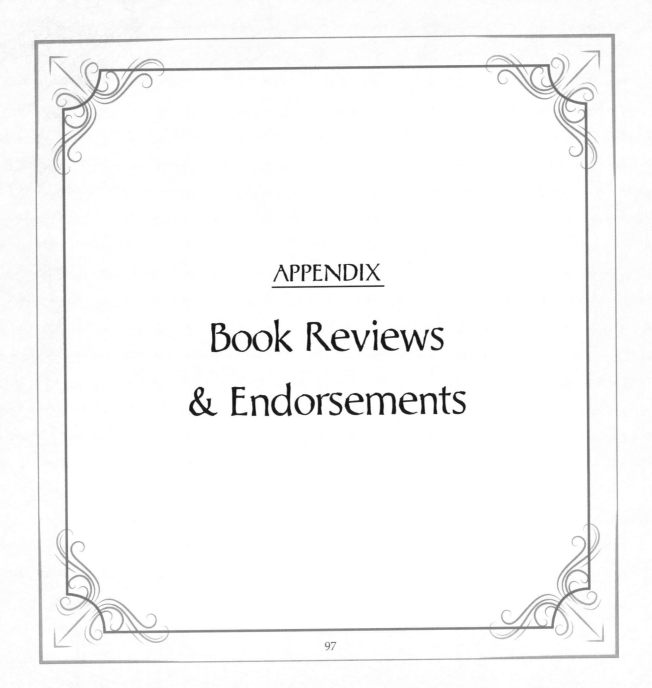

APPENDIX

Book Reviews
& Endorsements

A Heavenly Conversation One Night Before Christmas by Jennifer Lynn Heck envisions God's amazing plan of redemption from the vantage point of a divine conversation in heaven. This book reflects her creative imagination—taking you on a journey to the Christmas manger, the Easter cross and resurrection, and Jesus Christ's victorious second coming. Jennifer's story is based on the Bible and communicates basic doctrines that are vitally important to the Christian faith.

Jennifer is a spiritual giant to me. She has been tested by a lifetime of disability and limitations; yet she has a joyous, Christ-like spirit that I greatly admire. Jennifer's experience has enabled her to see God's Word through a different lens than most.

BOB RUSSELL, *Author and Retired Senior Pastor, Southeast Christian Church; Louisville, Kentucky*

This book is the greatest evangelism tool I have found. And I also enjoyed the heavenly conversations.

ESTHER JAGGERS; *Louisville, Kentucky*

Jennifer's gift is undeniable. She writes with a heart filled with wonder, a mind rooted in wisdom, and a life lived with grace. This book will open your eyes to the message of Christmas in a fresh way and challenge you to live out the power of this life-changing story.

KYLE IDLEMAN, *Author and Senior Pastor, Southeast Christian Church; Louisville, Kentucky*

I met Jennifer Heck years ago in a women's Bible study. She has an amazing love for the Lord and passion for people to see just how awesome He is. In this book the conversation between God the Father, Son, and Holy Spirit is heartwarming. I love the fact this book is for Christmas and Easter, for the young and old, for people who are believers and those who are seeking. It's a perfect gift as well.

DIANE YOUNG; *Prospect, Kentucky*

With a great heart for her Savior, Jennifer writes from a unique, interesting and creative slant! Her thoughts will intrigue and help motivate the reader to bow down and worship our great God—the Father, Son and Holy Spirit.

KURT SAUDER, *President, Further Still Ministries; Louisville, Kentucky*

*J*ennifer brings a unique perspective to the timeless Christmas story. Readers of her book will travel from eternity past to the first Christmas to the first Easter and beyond. Since her Bible-based story is set in the framework of a conversation among the persons of the Trinity, it will no doubt stir extra interest among readers with slightly different views on that subject.

Jennifer Heck is one of the most remarkable women I have ever known. Although having cerebral palsy, she has inspired thousands of people by the articles she has written.

DR. DAVID EUBANKS, *Author and Retired President, Johnson Bible College; Knoxville, Tennessee*

*W*ords cannot describe the heartfelt feeling I had when I first read the book. My wish is that I had the money to buy one for every family in our educational system. This book is awesome!! It is a message the world needs to hear. The author wrote in such an excellent way for everyone to understand!

KAY BROWN; *Carterville, Illinois*

*A*uthor Jennifer Lynn Heck combines her gifted writing skills with her contagious love for Jesus to present the Christmas story from a unique and thoughtful perspective. The foundational Biblical truths, along with the powerful message of the gospel make this a timeless book for all ages. What a wonderful gift idea! This book will continue to bless our family and allow us to bless others for years to come!

CHRISTIAN McCUTCHEON, *President, BrightStar Care; Louisville, Kentucky*

I love how this book keeps the main thing, the main thing—Jesus' mission and purpose to reconcile our relationship with God. It reveals the One and Only, Almighty and Powerful God, as a personal and approachable Heavenly Father who loves and cares deeply about you, your circumstances and your eternity.

The snapshots/picture section could be a great tool for sharing the gospel in a way that breaks through age and language barriers. The book will leave each person that reads it completely with the convicting question: "What will you do with the gift of Jesus?"

CAROL SCHICK; *Louisville, Kentucky*

MORE BOOK REVIEWS AT JJJHECK.COM

What will you do with the gift from which all blessings flow?